THE CHOSEN ONE(s)
a play about destiny(s)
{one-act special}

by David Andrew Laws

Uproar Theatrics

**LICENSING &
PRODUCTION INQUIRIES
Uproar Theatrics, LLC.
hello@uproartheatrics.com I www.UproarTheatrics.com**

The Chosen One(s): One-Act Special
© 2025 David Andrew Laws

The Chosen One(s) is published by Uproar Theatrics, LLC
500 8th Ave FRNT 3, #1714 New York, NY 10018

ISBN:978-1-968051-42-6

First Printing, January 2026

CHARACTERS

The Powers That Be
The Warden of The Past (PTB 1)
The Warden of The Present (PTB 2)
The Warden of That Which Is Yet to Come into Being but One Day Will (PTB 3)

The Chosen One(s)
The BOY WIZARD – an annoying and magical character legally distinct from Harry Potter
The BROODING HACKER – Neo meets John Nada meets Batman
The ASS-KICKING TEEN – Buffy Anne Summers meets Juliet Starling meets Rey Skywalker
The SILENT PROTAGONIST – Link meets The Courier meets Gordon Freeman
The RELUCTANT BLOND – Luke Skywalker meets Bruce Banner meets Frodo Baggins
The BRAVE VOLUNTEER – Katniss Everdeen meets Ellie Williams meets Wonder Woman
The SON OF THE GODS – Percy Jackson meets Hercules meets Thor

The Antagonists
The FANATIC – an obsessive creature with the energy of Gollum from The Lord of The Rings
The OVERTHINKER – a villainous force of destruction
The GRUNTS – nameless, indistinguishable cannon fodder
The RAVENOUS MAW – a monster in The OVERTHINKER's employ
The TOXIC TRIAD SISTERS – The OVERTHINKER's villainous trio of warriors
JEFF – a guy The OVERTHINKER paid twenty bucks to get in The Chosen Ones' way

<u>The Others</u>
The CUSTOMER – a customer and proud nerd
The MENTOR – Gandalf meets Obi Wan meets Merlin
The VENDOR – a vendor in the park selling magical goods

A Note on Casting – Diversity is good! Casting should reflect the talents and types in the room, not any preconceptions about race or gender that any of these roles might project. Characters should use and respect one another's stated pronouns, but can be played by anyone.

Other Notes –

- *sigh* <u>Yes</u>, the character of "The Ass-Kicking Teen" *can* be represented as "The Butt-Kicking Teen" where needed. It's not a <u>good</u> choice, but it's an available adjustment if wooing a prudish board member is the only way to get the show produced. In that vein, all instances of "ass" can be changed to butt for the aforementioned reason.
- Specificity of staging in this piece is, for the most part, a guideline. Lines, on the other hand, are very strictly structured: moments when characters have individualized lines are always important (except the ones that are for throwing away) and moments when characters speak simultaneously should be jumbled and indecipherable. There is even room for some ab libbing in these moments, as long as they maintain the spirit of the text.
- This show is all about pacing. It is the intersection of the traditional hero's journey cycle matched with the presentational energy of *The Play That Goes Wrong*. To an extent, all of the characters know they're characters presenting a story, and that impacts the way they interact with both the narrative and the audience, whether that's to try to lean into getting audience attention/reaction or fervently ignoring them and attempting to give an award-winning performance from behind their own fourth wall. In either case, everything is very real, and nothing should be pretended except for what is pretend.
- Dialogue in **bold** indicates emphasis by volume. <u>Underlined</u> dialogue indicates emphasis by tempo. The "//" symbol indicates an overlap in dialogue between characters or actions.

OUTLINE

SCENE I – a liminal space, in which our heroes are introduced

SCENE II – a comic book shop, in which the party is assembled and a villain is revealed

SCENE III – at the top of Mt. Mood, in which a Mentor is met

SCENE IV – a liminal space – in which the villain gains power

SCENE V – a comic book shop – in which the veil is broken

SCENE VI – inside The Overthinker's fortress – in which the true villain is revealed

Special Thanks to Isabella Greathouse, Giselle Muise, Sophia Carlin, Daniel Morrison, Michele Danna, Zaramaria Fas, Allison Wein, Maera Hagage, Lee (Emry) Sottile, Darcy Thompson, Gregory Petershack, Kyle Holmes, Laura Hall, and, ever and always, Alexandra Abney

SCENE I

A liminal space.

The stage is dark and blank. The curtain is down, if applicable. The air of awe and mystery is amplified by the technical design: a low rumble in the soundscape, a twinkling of lights, perhaps a light rolling fog – whatever can be done to foster an atmosphere of intrigue and oncoming adventure.

Assembled in the darkness are The BOY WIZARD, The BROODING HACKER, The RELUCTANT BLOND, The SILENT PROTAGONIST, The ASS-KICKING TEEN, The BRAVE VOLUNTEER, and The SON OF THE GODS arranged in a frozen tableau that will look totally super epic and cool once it is revealed. Each of them is striking their own character-defining pose, but the sum of their poses is even more awesome than their parts. We just can't see it yet.

The Powers That Be enter severally, each lit by a follow spot or a held light.

PTB 1
Before there was Time, there was…

PTB 1 *(simultaneously)* The Prophecy!
PTB 2. *(simultaneously)* The Prophecy!

PTB 3
(trying to be simultaneous, but a little bit late) The Prophecy!

(PTB 1 & PTB 2 shoot PTB 3 a look.)

1

PTB 3
Sorry.

PTB 1
(recovering the grandeur of the moment) And The Prophecy foretold evil. And The Prophecy foretold good. And The Prophecy foretold that a hero would rise so that a villain could fall.

PTB 2
The Prophecy told of a great journey: of reluctance and change, of thresholds and mentors, of trials and transformations, of death and rebirth.

PTB 3
And at the center of it all, The Prophecy foretold of…a chosen one!!

> *(The curtain rises, if applicable, and a light comes up on the group of Chosen Ones. The Powers That Be look between themselves and The Chosen Ones with confusion. The Chosen Ones aren't sure what to do with themselves. Some of them are better at hiding their confusion and concern, but they all keep it together more or less, just a few furtive glances here and there.)*

PTB 1
Wait, what?

> *(PTB1 counts the assembled Chosen Ones while PTB 2 looks ashamed and PTB 3 looks confused.)*

PTB 1

Seven?? Between the three of us, we elected <u>seven</u> avatars of destiny? We were supposed to pick **ONE**!

PTB 2

I didn't know we had to be unanimous, so I brought one and a back-up in case the first one beefed it.

PTB 3

Me too. That or, you know, sequel bait.

PTB 1

No, no, no! There's got to be **one** Chosen One. That's the way the trope goes. So let's…<u>choose</u> one so that the day can go on getting saved.

PTB 2

But which one?

PTB 1

Well, we've certainly got options. Let's see who we're playing with. We could choose…

> *(The Powers That Be turn back to the group of Chosen Ones.)*

PTB 1
(back in presenting voice) **The Silent Protagonist**!

> *(The SILENT PROTAGONIST steps forward. More likely does a big kick jump forward and makes a video-game-like effort noise.)*

SILENT PROTAGONIST

Hyyyah!

PTB 2

Not exactly silent.

PTB 1

He's not **mute**; he just doesn't **speak**. Makes him easier to connect with. In theory. *(brushing that line of thought aside)* But if you don't like him, what about… *(presenting)* **The Brave Volunteer**!

> *(The BRAVE VOLUNTEER moves forward, notches an arrow, and fires it offstage.)*

BRAVE VOLUNTEER

I'll do whatever it takes to protect my home and the family I love.

PTB 3

What's so special about <u>her</u>? They're <u>all</u> brave. They're answering the summons of a life-changing quest.

PTB 1

(confident throughout) Yes, but this one's *(reaching)* …a volunteer.

PTB 2

So she's not going to refuse the call to adventure?

PTB 1

I mean, she <u>is</u>, but then, she'll, like…volunteer to…– Shut up! Alright? Let's hear your suggestions if you're so smart.

PTB 2

Gladly. I propose…*(presenting)* **The Son of the Gods**!

> *(The SON OF THE GODS slides into position with the crash of a wave and a crack of lightning.)*

SON OF THE GODS

With the power of the heavens on my side, nothing will stand in my way!

(PTB 1 and PTB 3 are unimpressed. PTB 1 makes a fart noise with his mouth.)

PTB 3

That kid is, like, twelve.

PTB 2

He's seventeen!

PTB 1

And he seems <u>way</u> overpowered. What's his backstory?

PTB 2

(defensively) He's the son of Zeus! *(bashfully)* And Poseidon. *(rattling them off)* And Hades and Athena and Ares and Dionysus and Aphrodite from an alternate universe where they could all have a son together without it being weird.

PTB 1

Bit of a stretch.

PTB 2

Well, what if we go with… *(presenting)* **The Ass-Kicking Teen**.

(The ASS-KICKING TEEN takes CS with a roundoff or other gymnastic feat.)

ASS-KICKING TEEN

Vampires? Zombies? I'm more scared of failing my geometry midterm.

PTB 1
(impressed) That's some real final-girl energy.

PTB 2
(excited) And then, in a best-case scenario, Ass-Kicking Teen and The Son of the Gods have this "will-they, won't-they" chemistry that allows for a <u>very</u> engaging spin-off series, if you know what I mean.

PTB 1
Save it for your fan fiction. *(to PTB 3)* Who'd you choose?

PTB 3
(clearing their throat) Uhhhh, oh yeah! I brought forth…
The Reluctant Blond!

> *(The RELUCTANT BLOND steps into position with a slouch and a lot of hidden potential.)*

RELUCTANT BLOND
(whiny) But I was going into Smoshi Station to pick up some capacity transformers.

PTB 2
Whiny.

PTB 1
And blond. *(with the sub-text of 'remind me')* Why is that important?

PTB 3
Well–…

PTB 2
Yeah, does he have powers or…?

PTB 3

(self-conscious) I mean, he does…but they're, like, really under the surface, and they keep getting retconned and contextualized and…forget it, whatever. How about instead… *(presenting)* **The Brooding Hacker**.

> *(The BROODING HACKER steps forward, speaking through or overtop of outrageously-dark sunglasses.)*

BROODING HACKER

I'm here to hack computers and alter realities, and I'm all outta computers.

> *(PTB 1 and PTB 2 look back at PTB 3.)*

PTB 3

Yeah, I gotta admit, in a group project, I usually let you guys do all the heavy lifting.

PTB 2

I'll say.

PTB 1

But wait, if we each chose two, *(pointing at The BOY WIZARD)* then who's that?

> *(The BOY WIZARD moves DS of all of the other Chosen Ones.)*

BOY WIZARD

(with too much energy) I AM THE BOY WIZARD! I'M HERE TO STOP EVIL AND SAVE THE DAY USING MAGIC AND THE POWER OF FRIENDSHIP!

> *(The Powers That Be simultaneously jeer at The BOY WIZARD, chasing him off with their vitriol.*

Suggested lines are below, but they really lay into him, growing in intensity until he exits.)

PTB 1. *(simultaneous)* Oh my god, no, it's not about you. Learn to interpret ancient lore, you little–. Get outta here! We hate you!!
PTB 2 *(simultaneous)* Not this guy again. Gimmie a break. You don't even use your magic consistently. Scram, you little power creep!!
PTB 3. *(simultaneous)* No no no, I'm gonna break your wand in half and throw both bits into two different volcanoes if you don't get lost, you **loser**!!

(Once The BOY WIZARD leaves, The Powers That Be compose themselves.)

PTB 1
(to the audience) Sorry about that. *(back to the group)* So.

PTB 2
So.

PTB 3
I really hate that guy.

PTB 1
(quickly) I know, I know, I know. *(taking control)* But. We've got a world to save.

PTB 2
Well... *(of The Chosen Ones)* one of <u>them</u> does.

PTB 3
But which one?

PTB 1

I really can't stress how much danger the entirety of reality is in. Like, doomsday is <u>imminent</u>.

PTB 3

Maybe we just infuse all six of them with a lot of potential and…hope for the best.

(PTB 1 and PTB 2 consider this.)

PTB 1

You know, that's not your <u>worst</u> idea?

PTB 2

Sure, as long as only <u>one</u> person ends up saving the day, we've done our job!

PTB 1

And done it…well, not "well", but–

PTB 3

Well enough!

PTB 1

It'll have to do.

(PTB 1 turns back to the audience, leading the charge back into the presentational.)

PTB 1

(presenting) Prepare for a story only time can tell,

PTB 2

(presenting) On a journey new, though known quite well.

PTB 3

(presenting, but bad still) And now we are rhyming and isn't that swell?

PTB 1

Which heroes will rise, and which ones will fall?

PTB 2

Which plotlines will falter and which will stand tall?

PTB 3

Act wisely, Chosen Ones. We're counting on y'all.

PTB 1

Heroes. We grant you your potential. But your destinies are yours to fulfill. And your journey begins…

PTB ALL

NOW!

(The lights and sound rise into a tremendous din before crashing into a BLACKOUT!)

<u>SCENE II</u>

A comic book shop.

Your standard local game store with a front counter and various racks of comic books and other nerd paraphernalia. Not for nothing, longboxes are a great stand-in for seeing actual bulks of merchandise, but it would also be fun to see the fronts of various comic books (real or imagined) on display.

The RELUCTANT BLOND stands behind the counter in mid-confrontation with The SON OF THE GODS and The BRAVE VOLUNTEER. The CUSTOMER is standing somewhere in the background, leafing through a comic book. A bell dings SL as The SILENT PROTAGONIST, The ASS-KICKING TEEN, and The BROODING HACKER jump, flip, and saunter, respectively, into the room. The ASS-KICKING TEEN unfurls a scroll.

ASS-KICKING TEEN
This is the place! Time to get busy saving that damsel.

BROODING HACKER
(indicating The RELUCTANT BLOND) That guy doesn't look like a damsel, but he definitely looks like he needs saving.

SON OF THE GODS
(waving a scroll in The RELUCTANT BLOND'S face) What is the meaning of this, you flaxen-headed deceiver?

RELUCTANT BLOND
(swatting at the scroll, trying to catch it) If you'll just let me explain–...

BRAVE VOLUNTEER
(to The SON OF THE GODS) I knew teaming up was a mistake. I'm getting out of here and finding someone else to save. *(gravely)* Someone who really needs it....

RELUCTANT BLOND
Wait, but–!

ASS-KICKING TEEN
Iiiiis everything alright in here?

RELUCTANT BLOND
Yes, everything's fine. Welcome to– *(seeing the scroll in The ASS-KICKING TEEN'S hand)* Oh! You got my flyer too. *(with a quick survey of the room)* That puts us at a full six!

BROODING HACKER
Six what?

RELUCTANT BLOND
Adventurers! Now we can rescue The Damsel of Lucerna Lake.

ASS-KICKING TEEN
(striking a pose) That's right! We're here to help.

SILENT PROTAGONIST
Hyyah!

BRAVE VOLUNTEER
And who are you three supposed to be?

BROODING HACKER
We could ask you the same thing, sister.

BRAVE VOLUNTEER
(grabbing him by the lapels) How <u>dare</u> you mention my sister?

(The ASS-KICKING TEEN steps between them.)

ASS-KICKING TEEN
Alright, hands off the merchandise. We need him for now.

BROODING HACKER
Hey, I don't need anybody, so don't anybody start needing me! I'm a lone wolf and don't any of you forget it.

ASS-KICKING TEEN
Listen, if blondie says it'll take six of us to rescue the damsel, the six of us have to get along. For now.

SON OF THE GODS
I agree with she whose eyes sparkle like Time's first sunset.

(The ASS-KICKING TEEN blushes.)

SON OF THE GODS
No matter our motivations, if we are to rescue this maiden, then we <u>must</u> band together.

SILENT PROTAGONIST
(raising his sword aloft) Iyah!

SON OF THE GODS
For glory!

ASS-KICKING TEEN
For justice!

BROODING HACKER
For power!

BRAVE VOLUNTEER

For family!

RELUCTANT BLOND

Wow, I've never seen people so worked up to play a game before.

> *(The BROODING HACKER, The ASS-KICKING TEEN, The BRAVE VOLUNTEER, and The SON OF THE GODS deflate. The SILENT PROTAGONIST and The RELUCTANT BLOND stay as they are.)*

BROODING HACKER

To what now?

RELUCTANT BLOND

To play a game? Bards & Battlements. *(pulling out another scroll)* That's what th–...that's what we need six players for.

BROODING HACKER

Bards & Battlements? Is that like Dungeons & Dragons?

RELUCTANT BLOND

Well, we can't afford to carry official D&D products in the shop, so this is a...totally different dice-based roleplaying game.

ASS-KICKING TEEN

Oh, one of those nerd games for nerds? I'm not playing that.

BROODING HACKER

Sorry, I'm still trying to wrap my head around this. You called upon six strangers to play a <u>game</u>?

RELUCTANT BLOND

Well, yeah, the…my boss wants us to start hosting some events, so I was looking for other players to run a campaign with me.

BRAVE VOLUNTEER

There are no real, endangered damsels?

RELUCTANT BLOND

Not to my knowledge.

SON OF THE GODS

(grabbing The RELUCTANT BLOND by the lapels) Then <u>why</u> did you summon us in such a dramatic manner?

RELUCTANT BLOND

I dunno, I thought it would be immersive!

ASS-KICKING TEEN

(reading from the scroll) 'Calling all heroes, adventurers, and otherwise protagonists. The stars have foretold your arrival. Will you answer the call? Come rescue the Damsel of Lucerna Lake and claim your place in history. The fate of the story rests in your ready hands.' *(realizing she didn't read this part before; that makes more sense)* 'Bring your own snacks or something to share.'

BROODING HACKER

(grabbing The RELUCTANT BLOND's lapels alongside The SON OF THE GODS) But what about the reward?

RELUCTANT BLOND

Ten thousand gold pieces? That's in-game loot – our characters' reward for completing the quest. Did you think someone was actually offering gold pieces as currency? For what, some kind of rescue mission? That's not something that happens!

ASS-KICKING TEEN

Listen, pal, I've got a best friend who's a witch and a best friend whose soul is stuck in a vacuum cleaner, and we solve mysteries around the school with the help of a janitor with glowing green eyes. So don't tell me what kinds of things do and don't happen.

> *(The BRAVE VOLUNTEER grabs a comic book and holds it hostage.)*

BRAVE VOLUNTEER

Tell us the truth, book merchant, or it's curtains for this comic strip!

RELUCTANT BLOND

No! That's an original Shoebill Man Alpha Print Issue Number One.

SON OF THE GODS

It's about to be confetti if you don't start making this make sense.

RELUCTANT BLOND

No, please!

BROODING HACKER

Crease the front cover!

> *(As The RELUCTANT BLOND reaches full panic, the room starts to shake, a deep rumbling bass accompanying his words.)*

RELUCTANT BLOND

No, no, don't! I don't know what more to tell you! I'm just a nerd who works at a comic book store! I thought getting a group together for a team-based roleplaying game would

RELUCTANT BLOND (cont)
help me make some friends, but apparently I messed it up
just like I mess up everything in my life, and I'm sorry! I just
wanted to do like it says in the Bards & Battlements
handbook and make my life a story worth reading in a world
worth saving.

> *(A pause while this all sinks in, the shaking and
> rumbling fading away. The other Chosen Ones
> are aware of the rumbling and its departure. The
> BROODING HACKER and The SON OF THE
> GODS release The RELUCTANT BLOND.)*

SON OF THE GODS
How could I have been so brainless? I thought this was a
test. One step closer to joining my family on Mount
Olympus. But I'm no god. I'm no more than an ordinary
fool.

ASS-KICKING TEEN
(playfully teasing) Don't worry about it. I'm sure you're an
extraordinary fool. *(brushing off The RELUCTANT BLOND's
lapel)* Sorry about that.

SILENT PROTAGONIST
(confused at the change in the room's energy) Eeyah?

> *(The BRAVE VOLUNTEER tosses the comic
> book aside.)*

BROODING HACKER
(to The RELUCTANT BLOND) Next time you wanna make
friends, kid, stick to the internet.

> *(Suddenly, the shop is filled with noise and
> flashing lights. The room shakes as comic books*

*fall from their shelves. The Chosen Ones all
keep their footing, but the CUSTOMER in the
background falls over. Finally, everything stops
and the scene is silent and still.)*

CUSTOMER
(after a moment) **What the heck was that**??

*(The bell rings from the door SL as The
OVERTHINKER enters menacingly.)*

OVERTHINKER
(advancing on The Chosen Ones) There you are…gathered
together at last. *(waving dismissively at The CUSTOMER
without even looking at them)* <u>You</u> may go. *(pointing at The
Chosen Ones)* My business is with <u>them</u>.

CUSTOMER
…do I have to or…?

OVERTHINKER
(stopping; not what he was expecting) What?

CUSTOMER
(stammering) Y-you said I <u>could</u> go but I don't wanna go I'm
not done pickin' out my comics yet.

*(The OVERTHINKER ponders for a moment,
then waves a hand again.)*

OVERTHINKER
You may stay.

CUSTOMER
Thank you!

(The OVERTHINKER approaches the counter where The Chosen Ones have subconsciously arranged themselves into a protective little huddle.)

OVERTHINKER

Well, well, well. What. Have. We. <u>Here</u>?

(The Chosen Ones stand strong and each try to get in the first line of combative dialogue. None of their lines particularly stand out over the others. Sonically, it's just a mess.)

BROODING HACKER. *(simultaneous)* You walked into the wrong comic shop, pal–

ASS-KICKING TEEN. *(simultaneous)* Get a load of Mister Tall, Dark, and Not So Handsome–

SILENT PROTAGONIST. *(simultaneous)* Hrrrrrrrrrrrrrrrr–

RELUCTANT BLOND. *(simultaneous)* Listen, mister, we don't want any trouble–

BRAVE VOLUNTEER. *(simultaneous)* If you try to harm any innocents on my watch–

SON OF THE GODS. *(simultaneous)* Prepare to be stricken by the power of–

(The Chosen Ones realize they're talking over each other, look at each other, look back at The OVERTHINKER, then huddle up forming a semi-circle that excludes The OVERTHINKER but includes the audience.)

SON OF THE GODS

What are you doing?

BROODING HACKER

I was <u>trying</u> to get in a cheeky one-liner.

19

ASS-KICKING TEEN
Well, get in <u>line</u>, so was <u>I</u>.

RELUCTANT BLOND
You guys can go first. I was just gonna ask him to leave.

ASS-KICKING TEEN
Well, <u>one</u> of us has to jab him with a quick quip, or else what's the point?

BRAVE VOLUNTEER
Perhaps there is an equitable way to settle this.

SILENT PROTAGONIST
(raising a fist in offering) Hyah?

> *(The other Chosen Ones consider and then agree. They silently play a six-person game of Rock, Paper, Scissors, going on 'Rock, Paper, Scissor, Shoot'. The SON OF THE GODS shoots Rock, The BROODING HACKER shoots Scissors, The ASS-KICKING TEEN shoots Scissors, The RELUCTANT BLOND shoots Paper, The BRAVE VOLUNTEER shoots Paper, and The SILENT PROTAGONIST shoots Rock.)*

BROODING HACKER. *(simultaneous)* These are actually laser scissors that cut through rock and light paper on fire, so—
ASS-KICKING TEEN. *(simultaneous)* I once defeated a bigfoot with nothing but a pair of scissors, so I think—
SILENT PROTAGONIST. *(simultaneous)* Hyyyyyyyyah! Ha hup! Hyya!
RELUCTANT BLOND. *(simultaneous)* I knew this wasn't going to work with this many people, but maybe if we do—

BRAVE VOLUNTEER. *(simultaneous)* There is nothing more dangerous to systems of oppression than the power of paper, so—

SON OF THE GODS. *(simultaneous)* I created a rock so heavy that even I couldn't lift it, so obviously it should—

OVERTHINKER

Silence!!

> *(The Chosen Ones turn to face The
> OVERTHINKER, shocked into silence, except:)*

RELUCTANT BLOND

(from out of the dim; not having realized quickly enough) —
best two out of three… oh.

OVERTHINKER

I will tell you who I am. **I** am your doom. **I** am your demise.
I am The Overthinker!

> *(None of The Chosen Ones know quite how to
> react to this, so they don't. Or they do with a
> little confusion and titled heads.)*

OVERTHINKER

(caught off-guard that they're not reacting) What?

> *(The Chosen Ones look among themselves.
> Somehow The RELUCTANT BLOND gets
> volunteered as the next one to speak. He works
> here, after all.)*

RELUCTANT BLOND

Well, it's just…you say that like we're supposed to have
heard of you. And I don't think any of us have. Are you…a
band or something?

(That wasn't what he was supposed to say. The other Chosen Ones react with frustration.)

BROODING HACKER. *(simultaneous)* **How could a guy be a band**??
ASS-KICKING TEEN. *(simultaneous; sarcastically)* Very intimidating, big guy.
SILENT PROTAGONIST. *(simultaneous)* Hyyah! Huh! Hup!
RELUCTANT BLOND. *(simultaneous)* I'm sorry, I didn't know what to say–!
BRAVE VOLUNTEER. *(simultaneous)* That wasn't menacing at all!
SON OF THE GODS. *(simultaneous; praying)* If anyone's there, save me from these fools–

OVERTHINKER
Silence!!!

(The Chosen Ones are all successfully stunned into silence this time. The OVERTHINKER paces around them as he monologues.)

OVERTHINKER
(facetiously) Am I to understand that one of these <u>bickering fools</u> could alter the balance of the universe? How incredibly unlikely.

ASS-KICKING TEEN
(to the other Chosen Ones) I don't like the look of this guy.

BROODING HACKER
Don't get too close; I bet you wouldn't like the smell of him either.

OVERTHINKER

But here you are. In the flesh. And seeing you face-to-face like this, I wonder why I ever concerned myself with the likes of you. Small. Insignificant. And soon to be destroyed. I will wipe your names from the book of time as easily as I will wipe your bodies from the face of this planet.

SON OF THE GODS

You'll have to kill us first!

BRAVE VOLUNTEER

I think that's what he's implying.

OVERTHINKER

And here I thought there might be some risk in gathering you all. But no, it turns out the sum of your parts is even more incompetent than you were on your own.

ASS-KICKING TEEN

You gathered us?

SON OF THE GODS

And who are you calling uncompotent?

BROODING HACKER

Yeah, check your facts, pal. Blondie over here got us together.

OVERTHINKER

(severely) That's just what I wanted you to **think**. But The Overthinker can put a thought inside your head as easily as you can turn a tap. I planted the module within this very shop. I directed the wind to blow those scrolls into each of your paths. *(to The RELUCTANT BLOND)* Did you think you would ever be brave enough to commune with strangers in such a dramatic fashion without an outside influence? I crept inside your mind and inspired you to reach out, gave

OVERTHINKER (cont)
you every word to entice foolish heroes into action. Your
only contribution was... *(mocking)* 'Bring snacks or
something else to share.'

RELUCTANT BLOND
(realizing; of The Chosen Ones) ...and none of you did.

OVERTHINKER
But now that you are gathered, I will destroy you all and
have no more reason to fear The Prophecy.

> *(The Chosen One's collective ears perk up at
> this.)*

SON OF THE GODS
Prophecy?

RELUCTANT BLOND
What prophecy?

OVERTHINKER
The Prophecy, you know-nothings!

BROODING HACKER
Like, capital T, capital P, "The Prophecy?"

OVERTHINKER
Yes! An ancient story carved into the bones of the universe
that tells of rising strength...and calamitous downfall. The
blueprints of how I will destroy your world and become the
most powerful being in the universe!

CUSTOMER
(observing) That doesn't seem very fair.

(The OVERTHINKER whirls around on The CUSTOMER. The Chosen Ones watch as well.)

OVERTHINKER

Fair??

CUSTOMER

Well, yeah. You've got all this deep, cosmic knowledge, as well as a bunch of undefined powers. These just seem like six randos that ended up in the same comic book store.

(The Chosen Ones look among themselves a little insulted.)

CUSTOMER

You could at least even the playing field a little bit.

(The OVERTHINKER considers this.)

OVERTHINKER

Fine. *(to The CUSTOMER)* I'm going to regret letting you stick around, aren't I?

CUSTOMER

(with a shrug) Hm.

(The OVERTHINKER snaps his fingers and The Powers That Be enter.)

OVERTHINKER

Would you mind…doing the thing that you do. Vis-à-vis The Prophecy?

(The Powers That Be all look at The Chosen Ones)

PTB 1

Oh my god, did we not tell you guys about The Prophecy
before we sent you out on your adventure?

>*(The Chosen Ones all shake their heads, either
>simultaneously or in different varying rhythms.)*

PTB 2

Ah, jeez. Our bad.

PTB 3

Some puppeteers of fate we turned out to be. Let's do this!!

>*(The Powers That be get into a ready
>formation.)*

PTB 1

Before there was Time, there was…

PTB ALL

The Prophecy!

PTB 2

And so it was written–

PTB 3

And so it shall be!

>*(What follows as The Prophecy is spoken is the
>best audio/visual display your production can
>produce. Lights, sounds, projections – a flowing
>miasma that depicts the words, events, and
>emotions of The Prophecy in a way that
>underscores, underlines, and highlights its
>magnitude without drawing away from the
>words themselves. Or nothing and you can
>ignore this stage direction. Honestly, if the*

words can't portray what they're supposed to convey, what am I even doing here?)

PTB 1

For as long as there have been forces of creation, there have also been forces of destruction. One day there will arise a power not only capable of destruction, but able to end the very act of creation itself.

PTB 2

And against that power, a hero shall rise! The power will be known by its desire for silence. And the hero will be known by the company they keep.

PTB 3

And should that hero fail, the power will rule, and everything shall end.

RELUCTANT BLOND

Everything??

PTB ALL

(with finality) Everything.

PTB 1

And when the power shall first show its face, the true hero will falter.

PTB 2

But by their rising up, events shall be put into motion unseen and unknown.

PTB 3

A mountain must be climbed, both of earth and of the mind.

PTB 1

For a party shall be formed of strangers who become friends.

PTB 2
And they shall seek out a series of old men who shall aid in their efforts, each with a beard that is longer and whiter than the last.

PTB 3
And at the eleventh second of the eleventh minute of the eleventh hour of the eleventh day of the eleventh week of the eleventh month of the eleventh year of the eleventh era, The Chosen One shall emerge. And the day shall be well and truly saved.

PTB 1
So it was…

PTB 2
…is…

PTB 3
…and forever will be."

PTB 1
(breaking character a bit; to PTB 3) And, just to say it out loud, you're getting much better at this.

PTB 3
(genuinely but still presenting) Thank you.

PTB 2
This has been…

PTB ALL
The Prophecy!

(The display fades away as The Powers That Be exit, waving their arms mysteriously and making unknowable little noises.)

PTB 3

Good luck you guys, you got this….

OVERTHINKER

Happy now?

BROODING HACKER

Not entirely. I mean, that was a lot to process.

CUSTOMER

I mean, c'mon, you gotta give 'em time to process!

OVERTHINKER
(furiously at The CUSTOMER) **Will you stay out of this**???

(The CUSTOMER takes a step back, and The OVERTHINKER composes himself, turning back to The Chosen Ones.)

OVERTHINKER

Luckily for you, there is also some uncertainty about <u>which</u> of you is destined to "defeat" me. Rather than destroying all six of you and potentially setting the stage for my own ironic failure, I will bide my time.

(The OVERTHINKER casually picks up the original Shoebill Man alpha print number one.)

OVERTHINKER

For now, you may live, as I gather new information and further power. But heed my warning. Should any of you attempt to stand in my way…

(The OVERTHINKER tears the comic book in half slowly as he makes his final threat)

OVERTHINKER

I will destroy **all** of you, chosen or not.

(The OVERTHINKER lets the halves of the comic book fall as The RELUCTANT BLOND shrieks.)

RELUCTANT BLOND

Original Shoebill Man alpha print issue one, nooo!

(The OVERTHINKER swoops toward the SL doorway.)

OVERTHINKER

Stay out of my way "Chosen Ones," or you'll wish for so swift a demise.

(The OVERTHINKER exits with a whirl of his cape and another menacing laugh, the bell of the door ringing in his wake. There is a light rumble, perhaps the echo of laughter, before all is silent and still in the comic book shop once more. The CUSTOMER walks over to the counter.)

CUSTOMER

Wow, I'm really glad I stayed for that after all. What a show. *(digs in his pocket for money and pays for his comic books)* Sorry about your original Shoebill Man alpha print number one, that stinks. You guys have fun figuring out which one of you is The Chosen One and how to save the world. *(walking toward the door)* Man, I do not envy any of you.

(The CUSTOMER exits with another ring of the bell.)

BROODING HACKER
(slowly coming to terms with what just happened) One of
<u>us</u>…is The Chosen One.

BRAVE VOLUNTEER
Not just a hero.

ASS-KICKING TEEN
Not just a savior.

BROODING HACKER
The capital C, capital O, Chosen One.

RELUCTANT BLOND
I'm not sure about any of this….

SON OF THE GODS
(meaning himself) I mean, come on, I think we've got a
pretty good idea which one of us it is.

BROODING HACKER
We really don't. If <u>that</u> guy didn't know, it could be any of
us.

SILENT PROTAGONIST
Hyah, hup?

> *(The RELUCTANT BLOND has a proper freak
> out and splits from the group.)*

RELUCTANT BLOND
This is crazy!!

ASS-KICKING TEEN
Slow down, tiger. We're all in this together.

RELUCTANT BLOND

Not me! I'm not in anything with anyone! **You** guys can play savior all you want, but **my** life was perfectly normal until you all showed up. Comin' in here grabbin' people, sayin' snarky quips, rippin' comic books in half. That's not me! That's not what I do! I'm not a hero. I work retail!

> *(The BROODING HACKER, The ASS-KICKING TEEN, and The BRAVE VOLUNTEER share a look. They've all worked retail; they get it. The SILENT PROTAGONIST is blissfully unaware. The SON OF THE GODS is smarmily unaware.)*

SON OF THE GODS

So we leave him behind. You heard what The Overstinker said: at the end of the day, only one of us matters.

BRAVE VOLUNTEER

I think he's wrong. We all have a part to play in this.

BROODING HACKER

You'll be safer with us, kid, I can promise you that. If he finds you out there on your own, he might just pick you off for fun.

RELUCTANT BLOND

But, but–

> *(The ASS-KICKING TEEN puts a hand on The RELUCTANT BLOND's shoulder.)*

ASS-KICKING TEEN

Hey. You can trust us. Life's thrown me its fair share of curveballs too. I've broken curses, thwarted alien invasions – I even tried out for the cheerleading team with a twisted ankle, and you know what happened?

RELUCTANT BLOND

How would I know // what–?

ASS-KICKING TEEN

(interrupting) I made the team. Because my friends distracted the judges and made it look like I did the best. I guess what I'm trying to say is: it takes a lot of girls to make a human pyramid, but there's only room for one at the top. Will you at least stick around and be a body we can climb on?

RELUCTANT BLOND

I uh…

ASS-KICKING TEEN

It's like you said: Let's make your life a story worth reading in a world worth saving.

(This fills The RELUCTANT BLOND with the resolve he needs.)

RELUCTANT BLOND

Okay. I'll do it.

BRAVE VOLUNTEER

That's the spirit!

SON OF THE GODS

Fine. More human shields for me.

BROODING HACKER

(to The ASS-KICKING TEEN) Hell of a pep talk.

SILENT PROTAGONIST

Hyeh! Ha?

BROODING HACKER

(of The SILENT PROTAGONIST) He's right, I think. Sounds like we've got a mountain to climb.

BRAVE VOLUNTEER

But which mountain? I volunteer to choose a mountain!

ASS-KICKING TEEN

What was it The Prophecy said? "And they shall seek out a series of old men who shall aid in their efforts–"

RELUCTANT BLOND

"–each with a beard that is longer and whiter than the last." Hey, yeah!

SON OF THE GODS

Okay, well, anyone got directions to a wise old man with a long white beard who lives at the top of a mountain?

(The bell above the door dings again as The FANATIC slinks onstage.)

FANATIC

I know where to look.

(The Chosen Ones react to this sudden presence, especially The SILENT PROTAGONIST who starts rolling and jumping up, leaping into various offensive and defensive poses.)

SILENT PROTAGONIST

Hiyup ha! Hyup! Hah! Hyah!

(The other Chosen Ones calm The SILENT PROTAGONIST.)

BRAVE VOLUNTEER
(to The SILENT PROTAGONIST) Stay your blade. Let's hear him out.

SON OF THE GODS
(to The FANATIC) Who or what are you?

FANATIC
Me, sweetness? <u>Ahem</u>. We are– <u>ahem</u>, sorry, <u>ahem</u>, was having pizza earlier, crust caught in throat. <u>Ahem, ahem</u>!

SON OF THE GODS
We shall call you Ahem.

FANATIC
What? No, that's not–...

BROODING HACKER
Cut to the chase, Ahem. What do you know about a bearded old man who lives on a mountain?

FANATIC
Yesssssss… Big beard. Big white beard. Very wise. Lives at the top of Mount Mood, he does. We can take you to him, sweetness! <u>Ahem</u>! <u>Ahem</u>!

BRAVE VOLUNTEER
What's in it for you?

FANATIC
Nothing, sweetness. We just wants to go on an adventure. Climb up the mountain to see the wise old man – that's adventure, sweetness.

SON OF THE GODS
That's a walk in the park for us.

ASS-KICKING TEEN
Not if we don't know where we're going.

BROODING HACKER
Why don't you just tell us where he is and we'll find our own way there?

FANATIC
Too dangerous, sweetness! Many trials, many enemies. But we know lots of secret shortcuts. We will get you there safely! <u>Ahem</u>!

BRAVE VOLUNTEER
And how do you know such a clear path? Why don't you volunteer to make us a map?

FANATIC
Can't remember off top of my head, sweetness. Only recognize the way by seeing it, <u>ahem</u>. Have to travel <u>with</u> you.

ASS-KICKING TEEN
I don't know about this....

BROODING HACKER
And I thought blondie was supposed to be the reluctant one.

RELUCTANT BLOND
Hey!

BROODING HACKER
Well, no offense, but I don't exactly see you offering any alternatives.

RELUCTANT BLOND

(to the other Chosen Ones) Don't you see? This has to be some kind of trap. *(of The FANATIC)* Either he has ulterior intentions or following him will hamper our journey and our personal developments. What if we're not ready to face The Overthinker when we find him because we took the first shortcut that presented itself? Shouldn't we tackle our own obstacles? Overcome our own challenges? Rise above our own preconceptions of what we're capable of?

(The other Chosen Ones consider this.)

BROODING HACKER

…nnnno, I think we should go with the guy who knows where he's going.

ASS-KICKING TEEN. *(simultaneous)* Yeah, I'm with the brooding one on this.
SILENT PROTAGONIST. *(simultaneous)* Hup hyah. Hup!
BRAVE VOLUNTEER. *(simultaneous)* There will be time for adversity later, frail one.
SON OF THE GODS. *(simultaneous)* No pain, much gain, my fathers always said.

(The RELUCTANT BLOND inhales.)

RELUCTANT BLOND

Alright. Lead the way, Ahem.

FANATIC

Yes! Yes! We will lead the way, sweetness! Up the mountain and into the maw of adventure. But not over his sharp little teethsies, sweetness. Up, up! Follow, follow! Ahem! Ahem!

> *(The FANATIC leads The Chosen Ones offstage left. The exiting order is something like The FANATIC, The SILENT PROTAGONIST, The*

*BRAVE VOLUNTEER, The SON OF THE
GODS, The BROODING HACKER, with The
ASS-KICKING TEEN and The RELUCTANT
BLOND lingering in the back of the group.)*

ASS-KICKING TEEN
*(putting an arm around The RELUCTANT BLOND's
shoulder)* See? You're starting to get a hang of this
adventuring thing.

RELUCTANT BLOND
I guess so.

ASS-KICKING TEEN
What better way forward could there possibly be? You'll see.

RELUCTANT BLOND
I hope you're right.

*(The ASS-KICKING TEEN exits. The
RELUCTANT BLOND turns and takes one last
longing look at the shop. He inhales and exits,
the bell ringing behind him. There is a moment
of stillness before The VENDOR enters through
the door with a tray full of items, like at a
baseball game.)*

VENDOR
World-saving items here! Get your magical, mystical, world-
saving items here! Can't carpe a diem without a deus ex
machina! Get 'em while they're guaranteed to alter the
course of destiny! No genies' curses, no monkey's paw
loopholes, just clean and fresh world-saving items here! First
one's free, get 'em while they're here. *(looks around at the
empty stage)* Huh. No one's here? Guess I'll go throw these
in a well. Oh well. *(realizing)* Ha. I see what I did there. Well
well. Well well well.

(The VENDOR continues muttering to himself as he exits SL and the lights fade to a Blackout.)

SCENE III

At the mouth of a cave atop Mount Mood.

SL is the entrance to The Cave. It is wide and imposing, decorated with stalactites and/or stalagmites as you see fit. The large playing area in front of the mouth of the cave gives the impression of height, as at the top of a mountain.

The Chosen Ones and The FANATIC enter SR.

FANATIC

This is the place, sweetness. See? Easy journey. Easy peasey. Ahem!

BROODING HACKER

Two days of uninterrupted travel. Good job, Ahem. We owe you one.

ASS-KICKING TEEN

And in that time, we've grown closer as people.

SON OF THE GODS

As teammates.

ASS-KICKING TEEN
(to The RELUCTANT BLOND) See? Worth it.

RELUCTANT BLOND

I still think it would have been more satisfying to share that growth with others somehow....

BRAVE VOLUNTEER
(to The FANATIC) So, where is he? Where's the bearded old wise man?

FANATIC
(pointing toward the cave) In there, sweetness. Lives in the cave. Allllll the way at the back.

RELUCTANT BLOND
Now <u>I've</u> got a bad feeling about this.

SON OF THE GODS
Oh, come now, he who trembles like the newborn calf. What could possibly go wrong?

> *(From out of the cave explodes an army of GRUNTS!, at least six, but ideally one or two dozen. Creative costuming or cardboard doubles can help increase the numbers, but our heroes should feel really overwhelmed by this attack.*
>
> *The Chosen Ones spring into action, defending themselves against The GRUNTS as much as possible as The GRUNTS use their superior numbers to their advantage. The scuffling that's not in the foreground can be kept to restrained shuffling or punch-block combos until it's that Chosen One's time to shine. The FANATIC watches from the sidelines, their glee becoming distress as The Chosen Ones gain the upper hand.*
>
> *First, The ASS-KICKING TEEN handily dispatches two or more grunts with an impressive gymnastic display. Then The SON OF THE GODS uses his god-given powers to dispatch a few more. They kick ass back-to-back for a little bit.)*

SON OF THE GODS
Your fighting technique is almost as beautiful as you are.

ASS-KICKING TEEN

Thanks. Ten years of ballet, eight years of tae kwon do, and thirteen summers of horse-riding camp will do that for ya.

> *(They smile at each other. Focus shifts to The BROODING HACKER. He's fending them off as best he can, maybe hacking one of them with a portable computer, but another is about to get him from behind, oh no! Suddenly, The BRAVE VOLUNTEER rescues him by shooting The GRUNT with an arrow! The BROODING HACKER sees that he was saved and then sees who saved him.)*

BROODING HACKER

Thanks, but I can handle myself.

BRAVE VOLUNTEER

Until we know which one of us is The Chosen One, I've got your back whether you like it or not!

> *(They fend off a few more before focus shifts to The SILENT PROTAGONIST and The RELUCTANT BLOND.*
>
> *The RELUCTANT BLOND is mostly cowering and ducking, his attempts to flee leading GRUNTS right into The SILENT PROTAGONIST's attacks. Eventually, while The SILENT PROTAGONIST is engaged, two or more GRUNTs gang up on The RELUCTANT BLOND, who panics. In a moment of sheer desperation, The RELUCTANT BLOND lets loose a powerful scream and flexes his hand at one of the GRUNTs, uses his latent mind powers to lift it off the ground. The GRUNT struggles in*

*the air and the rest look on in amazement. The
RELUCTANT BLOND howls as he flings the
GRUNT around for a bit before tossing him
offstage with a mighty crash. The Chosen Ones
are awe-struck, still struggling against the
GRUNTs, but focusing on what just happened.)*

BROODING HACKER
What was that??

RELUCTANT BLOND
I don't know…but it felt awesome!!

*(The fighting continues, everyone all at once. The push and
pull goes back and forth, but The GRUNTs are once more
getting the upper hand.)*

ASS-KICKING TEEN
(calling out in desperation) Ahem! Do something!

FANATIC
Ooh, sorry, sweetness. No can do. The Grunts want to eat
meat, and we provides it for a price.

BROODING HACKER
What?? Ahem, you little traitor!

FANATIC
That's not our name, sweetness! Our name is–!

*(A cosmic boom emanates from the mouth of the
cave as The MENTOR emerges, staff in hand.)*

MENTOR
(raising his staff) YOU SHALL NOT… *(slamming his staff
down)* DO THAT ANYMORE!

*(The GRUNTs are knocked off their feet! The
Chosen Ones remain upright, but just barely.
The bodies of any manufactured GRUNTs can
remain onstage as the rest retreat. The Chosen
Ones watch in awe as The MENTOR approaches
The FANATIC who recoils in fear.)*

MENTOR
How dare you darken my doorstep, you miserable creature.

FANATIC
Sorry, sir. No harm meant, sweetness. Was just bringing
these heroes to see you, <u>ahem</u>!

MENTOR
And who directed these Grunts to my cave as well, hm?
Thought you'd kill seven birds with a few dozen stones, did
you?

FANATIC
We don't know what you're talking about, sweetness. Must
have misheard us, <u>ahem</u>.

*(The MENTOR raises his staff against The
FANATIC. The FANATIC flinches and The
Chosen Ones react with shock. The MENTOR
lowers his staff and knocks against The
FANATIC's head twice.)*

MENTOR
Two for flinching.

*(Everyone relaxes a bit, but the mood is still
tense and dangerous.)*

MENTOR

If I see you again, I'll turn you into a toad with crippling student loan debt.

(The FANATIC panics and flees. Satisfied, The Mentor turns back to The Chosen Ones.)

MENTOR

Now. I don't remember leaving a welcome mat at my secluded cave entrance. What are you all doing here?

BROODING HACKER. *(simultaneous)* Listen here, gramps, we've come a long way in a short amount of time to–
ASS-KICKING TEEN. *(simultaneous)* We're the answer to your problems and everybody else's so you'd better–
SILENT PROTAGONIST. *(simultaneous)* Hyaaaaaaah ha! Ha! Hyup ha!
RELUCTANT BLOND. *(simultaneous)* Sorry to disturb you, it's just we've really got to figure out this capital C capital O business–
BRAVE VOLUNTEER. *(simultaneous)* We are here to learn at your feet, if you be the one we seek–
SON OF THE GODS. *(simultaneous)* The glory you see before you in none other than the savior of this and many worlds–

(The MENTOR raises a hand, and The Chosen Ones stop speaking. The MENTOR holds up one finger, indicating that only one of them should speak. The Chosen Ones look among themselves and volunteer The ASS-KICKING TEEN to step forward.)

ASS-KICKING TEEN

We're looking for a wise old man with a beard longer and whiter than that of Zeus himself to be our guide. Do you know him?

MENTOR.
Of course I know him. You're lookin' at him.

BROODING HACKER
We need your help. One of us is The Chosen One.

MENTOR
Capital C, capital O?

SON OF THE GODS
That's right. We just learned about The Prophecy.

MENTOR
Capital T, capital P?

BRAVE VOLUNTEER
Yes. Will you volunteer to help us?

MENTOR
Capital N, capital O.

*(The MENTOR turns and starts walking back
toward the mouth of The Cave.)*

BROODING HACKER
(taking a moment to understand) Wh–...wait, <u>no</u>?? What do
you mean, no?

(The MENTOR turns back.)

MENTOR
Guys, I live in a cave. I'm old. I got creepy little guys
bringin' all kindsa little googahs around my place. I'm <u>old</u>. I
just wanna be left in peace so I don't have to die and come
back in a different form.

RELUCTANT BLOND
Is that what happens when you die?

MENTOR
Not <u>you</u>. That's what happens when <u>I</u> die. I'm super old and magical and stuff, so when I die I'll come back in a new form, with a new name, and then I gotta change, like, all my driver's licenses and stuff. It's a big hassle. If one of <u>you</u> dies, you're just dead. And I don't wanna be a part of that either.

ASS-KICKING TEEN
But we've come a long way just to see you!

MENTOR
Did you? Or did you follow that freak up the shortcut side of the mountain? Name one peril you faced along the way. One lesson you learned?

(The Chosen Ones are embarrassed that they can't think of anything.)

MENTOR
Yeah, I didn't think so. The <u>real</u> Chosen One is probably out there right now making allies and thwarting enemies, not skating by on the <u>presumption</u> of greatness. *(turning to go)* Good day.

BROODING HACKER
(turning to go) Come on, guys–

MENTOR
(turning back; fiercely) **I said 'Good day!'**

BROODING HACKER
(turning back) I **know**! That's why we're **leaving**!

MENTOR

Oh. Sorry, most people…usually push back a little more.

BROODING HACKER

No, you win. Enjoy your cave. *(turning to go; to the other Chosen Ones)* Come on, guys. We'll find someone with a longer, whiter beard.

MENTOR

Wait!

(The Chosen Ones stop in their tracks and turn back.)

MENTOR

(gravely) …say that again.

BROODING HACKER

(smirking) Oh yeah, didn't we mention? You're not the only wizened old fart out there.

ASS-KICKING TEEN

(quoting) "And they shall seek out a <u>series</u> of old men who shall aid in their efforts…"

RELUCTANT BLOND

(finishing up) "…each with a beard that is longer and whiter than the last."

BRAVE VOLUNTEER

There could be hundreds of other mentors out there for us to find.

SON OF THE GODS

Dozens even.

BRAVE VOLUNTEER
(aside to The SON OF THE GODS) That's less than what I said.

SON OF THE GODS
(not getting it) Yeah! That's <u>less</u> than what she said!

SILENT PROTAGONIST
Hup, ha!

MENTOR
You really do know The Prophecy, eh?

BROODING HACKER
Every word.

SON OF THE GODS
'Bring snacks or something else to share.'

ASS-KICKING TEEN
(wrong prophecy) No, that's not–. Never mind.

BROODING HACKER
One of us is destined. For greatness. For <u>something</u>. And we're not going to stop until we find the right bearded old man. *(to The MENTOR)* So you can either rot away here in your little cave, alone and ineffective, frightened of your own transformation, or you can get off your magical dumper and be a partner of greatness.

> *(The MENTOR is shaking with fury. After a moment, he turns and storms off into The Cave. The Chosen Ones sigh with regret – they really thought they had him.)*

BROODING HACKER
Well–

(The MENTOR explodes back into the room with a blast of sound and light. He is carrying way more than he ought to be able to: weapons, artifacts, schematics, and he dumps them all majestically out in front of him.)

MENTOR
Who's ready to save the world??

(The Chosen Ones all cheer. The MENTOR starts passing out weapons and artifacts to the party as he lectures them.)

MENTOR
Rule number one: know thy enemy. Who we goin' up against?

SON OF THE GODS
The villain calls himself The Overthinker.

MENTOR
Ooh, hate to hear it – that guy's gonna be one step ahead of us the whole time. Anybody know the weakness of an overthinker?

ASS-KICKING TEEN
Anti-anxiety medication?

MENTOR
Close. <u>Under</u>thinking. Gut instinct. You're gonna do what you do best and that should be enough to bring you face-to-face.

RELUCTANT BLOND
But shouldn't we grow and change as a part of our journey? I just learned I've got some kind of…latent telekinetic ability.

MENTOR

And how did you manifest it?

RELUCTANT BLOND

Well, I don't know, I just…did.

MENTOR

Exactly! I don't want to undercut the work you've got to do, but at the end of the day, you've got to trust in yourselves and trust in each other. How long have you all known each other?

BRAVE VOLUNTEER

Not long at all, but already some of us are starting to feel like family.

MENTOR

Careful with that. He could use those feelings against you. Put one of you in danger as leverage against the others. Force you to make a deal of impossible choices. That's the kind of work overthinkers do.

BROODING HACKER

So we should stay emotionally distant. *(He likes the sound of that.)*

MENTOR

(correcting him) Can't do that either. If you're not a cohesive unit, he'll pry at your individual weaknesses until he manages to turn you all against each other. Squabbling, in-fighting, other third-act conflicts. What you've got to do is be true to yourselves and stick together. Whichever one of you is The Chosen One will reveal itself in time. Do I make myself clear?

(The SILENT PROTAGONIST gives a solemn nod.)

MENTOR
Good, now take these tools and triumph! Find and defeat each of The Overthinker's three underbosses – that'll lead you straight to his fortress. *(parenthetically)* He's a dangerous adversary, but not a terribly original thinker. *(no longer parenthetically)* By the time you face him, you should have found enough growth and developed enough character to stop this fiend for good. Now, get outta here, and be better than you've ever been before!

RELUCTANT BLOND
Aren't you coming with us?

MENTOR
I can't! *(gesturing to the cave mouth)* If those Grunts come back, they could use the rest of this arsenal to <u>really</u> wreak some havoc. Besides, <u>I'm</u> not The Chosen One. *(proudly)* One of <u>you</u> is. Now… *(waving his arms and shooing them off)* Fly, you geese!

(As The Chosen Ones exit, they give a battle cry. The MENTOR holds The BROODING HACKER back for a moment with his words.)

MENTOR
And thank you…for reminding me what it feels like to do something useful.

BROODING HACKER
Don't mention it, old timer.

(The BROODING HACKER turns to go. The MENTOR stops him again.)

MENTOR

And one more thing…if you do find someone else out there
with a longer, whiter beard than mine…don't tell me.

*(The BROODING HACKER chuckles and nods,
and exits. The MENTOR stands alone for a
moment, watching them leave. The
OVERTHINKER enters from The Cave.)*

OVERTHINKER

You can't stop me, you know.

MENTOR

Oh, I know. But one of them can. Someone should have a
long time ago.

OVERTHINKER

Why don't you do something about it now?

MENTOR

Because you're not real. You're not here right now. You
never were. Father.

OVERTHINKER

What?

(The MENTOR turns.)

MENTOR

Oh, sorry, I thought you were someone else.

OVERTHINKER

Why don't you leave the thinking to me?

*(A blade bursts through The MENTOR as The
OVERTHINKER runs him through. The
MENTOR is shocked, but accepts his fate as he*

dies. The OVERTHINKER laughs as The MENTOR slumps to the ground and falls. Blackout.)

SCENE IV

A liminal space.

The mouth of The Cave is gone. We're in a new liminal space, where the design indicates the passage of space and time: moving lights, warping sounds, etc. – it's a montage.

The Powers That Be enter and take positions around the stage. As they speak, The Chosen Ones enter and move through the space, as a clump, as a line, as a unit, enacting travel and the actions that The Powers That Be describe.

PTB 1
And so it was that The Chosen Ones set out to test themselves against the forces that would stand against them.

PTB 2
They used their inherent strengths, bolstered by The Mentor's wisdom and the skills of their partners, to defeat many enemies.

PTB 1
They struck down the Ravenous Maw, a feral beast in the Overthinker's employ.

(The Chosen Ones fight and defeat The RAVENOUS MAW. It is a thrilling fight.)

PTB 2
They defeated The Overthinker's mightiest warriors, The Toxic Triad Sisters.

(The Chosen Ones fight and defeat The TOXIC TRIAD SISTERS. It is a perilous fight.)

PTB 3

They fought some guy named Jeff that The Overthinker paid twenty bucks to get in their way.

(The Chosen Ones fight JEFF. It is…an embarrassing fight.)

PTB 1

And with their foe's underbosses defeated, they were brought to the lair of The Overthinker himself.

PTB 2

But even if they could breach his unrelenting fortress, they would not find their foe within.

PTB 1

No, for this destructive antagonist had been busy, growing in power and murdering mentors.

PTB 3

And now he meant to disrupt the very fabric of time by siphoning the energy of The Powers That Be themselves. PTB 1. *(did not see that coming)* Wait, what?

(The OVERTHINKER enters cackling and launches himself at The Powers The Be. Beams from his fingertips sap the energy from them as they writhe in agony.)

OVERTHINKER

Good to see you again! Or should I say, good to **be** you!!

(The OVERTHINKER cackles.)

PTB 1

How is this happening?

PTB 2

We never should have taken down that fourth wall!

> *(As The OVERTHINKER monologues, The Chosen Ones huddle together center stage, sensing an oncoming evil. They are not seeing or hearing what The OVERTHINKER is doing or saying, but they can feel a change in the wind. The design elements can help with this, as shadows creep closer and closer to their huddle.)*

OVERTHINKER

With your powers bolstering my own designs, I will ensure that no Chosen One shall rise against me. I will destroy what has been built. Only **I** will succeed, only **I** will remain! And **nothing** can stand in my way!!

> *(As The OVERTHINKER's laughter fills the space, the lights go out on him and The Powers That Be. The laughter and daunting music overwhelm as the shadows reach The Chosen Ones. They cannot fight them back and are soon engulfed in a Blackout.)*

SCENE V

A comic book shop.

Everything is very normal. The comic book shop is normal, the atmosphere is normal, even the characters onstage are normal. The Chosen Ones are gathered comfortably and eclectically, Breakfast Club-*style, around the front counter. They have paper, pencils, and dice scattered around them. The RELUCTANT BLOND sits in a centralized location behind a GM screen: they are at the tail end of a game of Bards & Battlements. They are not dressed in their full-on archetype costumes but look much more... normal. Normal people. In a normal place. Doing normal things.*

As the scene settles, we maybe see them silently go through a moment or two of gameplay. Then we see The ASS-KICKING TEEN roll a d20.

ASS-KICKING TEEN

Nat twenty!

RELUCTANT BLOND

Critical hit! Roll for damage.

ASS-KICKING TEEN

(checking her sheet) What's my damage?

SON OF THE GODS

(teasingly) Great question.

BROODING HACKER

(leaning to look at her sheet) With your battleaxe?

ASS-KICKING TEEN

Yeah. Both hands.

BROODING HACKER

(pointing) 1d10 plus…

ASS-KICKING TEEN

Three. *(checking with The RELUCTANT BLOND)* Yeah?

(The RELUCTANT BLOND nods proudly.)

BRAVE VOLUNTEER

(chiming in) And double the amount on the die because it's a critical hit, right?

RELUCTANT BLOND

Yep! You guys are really picking this up.

SON OF THE GODS

(surprised at how much fun they're having) We really are.

SILENT PROTAGONIST

Isn't it weird that we've only known each other for an afternoon?

> *(Everyone looks at The SILENT PROTAGONIST. We, the audience, should think they're looking at him because he spoke, and that is odd. But they're also coming to terms with the fact that it feels like they've known each other for a lot longer than that. Days, even. Haven't they? Wait a minute.)*

BROODING HACKER

…yeah. That is weird.

ASS-KICKING TEEN
(to The RELUCTANT BLOND) Eleven damage.

RELUCTANT BLOND
(returning to the game; making a note on his paper) Great!
You strike the bugbear in the side and with a final spurt of
blood, he falls! The remaining grablins have their morale
shaken and turn to flee. Will you pursue them or let them go?

BRAVE VOLUNTEER
We should chase after them! Before they have a chance to
regroup!

BROODING HACKER
It could be a trap. They know this forest way better than we
do.

SON OF THE GODS
Then let's split up. Flank them!

SILENT PROTAGONIST
This isn't right.

*(Everyone looks at The SILENT PROTAGONIST
again. The SILENT PROTAGONIST is
examining the fourth wall.)*

RELUCTANT BLOND
(checking behind the GM screen) Is it not? *(to The ASS-
KICKING TEEN)* You said two hands, right? Cause if
you've still got your shield up, it would only be 1d<u>8</u>.

ASS-KICKING TEEN
No, I–

SILENT PROTAGONIST
(meaning the game) Not that. *(meaning reality)* This.

SON OF THE GODS

What?

SILENT PROTAGONIST

All of this. Something's wrong.

BROODING HACKER

Come back to the game, man. We were just about to level up. *(to The RELUCTANT BLOND)* Weren't we?

RELUCTANT BLOND

No.

SILENT PROTAGONIST

We <u>were</u> about to level up. We were on the precipice of something great. A threshold that, once we'd crossed, we would never come back from. But something happened.

RELUCTANT BLOND

Oh no, I've seen this before. He's got roleplaying game madness. *(approaching The SILENT PROTAGONIST like a startled horse)* **<u>You</u> <u>are</u> <u>not</u> <u>your</u> <u>character</u>**.

SILENT PROTAGONIST

(wheeling on him with some fury) That's just it! I **<u>am</u>** a character. *(back into the middle distance)* A prototypical representation of something bigger and older than myself. I am the ancestral history of generations of hunters, gatherers, and storytellers that came before me. Before any of us. *(to the group)* Don't you see? **<u>This</u>** is the mask. Our true selves have been hidden.

ASS-KICKING TEEN

You're scaring me.

SILENT PROTAGONIST
(taking her by the shoulders) Good! Let that fear rattle around inside of you and shake you loose. *(to the group)* What's the last thing you all remember?

BROODING HACKER
We–...we were ambushed by a group of grablins and a handful of bugbear commanders.

SILENT PROTAGONIST
Not in the game. A <u>real</u> thing. Something real.

BRAVE VOLUNTEER
Weeee all sat down to play B&B together?

SILENT PROTAGONIST
Why?

SON OF THE GODS
Because we answered the summons. *(of The RELUCTANT BLOND)* The one <u>he</u> sent out.

SILENT PROTAGONIST
Not him. He gathered us. But because of whose influence?

BROODING HACKER
Because of The– AAGHH!

> *(The BROODING HACKER cries out in pain.*
> *The rest look on in fear.)*

BROODING HACKER
...the–

> *(The Chosen Ones are all struck with a terrible*
> *pain, a spike through their minds. They cannot*
> *think the name, let alone say it.)*

ASS-KICKING TEEN

What's happening?

SILENT PROTAGONIST

We weren't always playing this game. In reality, we never started.

(A bell rings as The BOY WIZARD enters SL. But he's just a normal guy.)

BOY WIZARD

(normally) Do you guys have the new Spider-Man in stock?

RELUCTANT BLOND

NO! WE'RE CLOSED! GET OUTTA HERE!

BOY WIZARD

Alright, jeez!

(The BOY WIZARD scurries away and exits.)

RELUCTANT BLOND

We never started playing Bards & Battlements. We were here. Learning about our destiny.

SON OF THE GODS

(realizing) And The Prophecy.

BROODING HACKER. *(simultaneous)* Capital T, capital P.
ASS-KICKING TEEN. *(simultaneous)* Capital T, capital P.
SILENT PROTAGONIST. *(simultaneous)* Capital T, capital P.
RELUCTANT BLOND. *(simultaneous)* Capital T, capital P.
BRAVE VOLUNTEER. *(simultaneous)* Capital T, capital P.
SON OF THE GODS. *(simultaneous)* Capital T, capital P.

(They are all shaken by their simultaneousness.)

BRAVE VOLUNTEER
Then we followed that creature up the mountain where we fought The Grunts–

ASS-KICKING TEEN
–and met a man with a long, white beard.

SILENT PROTAGONIST
He equipped us.

BROODING HACKER
Inspired us.

RELUCTANT BLOND
And from there, we fought. We grew. We triumphed.

RELUCTANT BLOND
Then what happened?

BRAVE VOLUNTEER
We rested.

ASS-KICKING TEEN
Despite the danger.

SON OF THE GODS
We went into the forest.

BROODING HACKER
And made a fire.

> *(A fire appears downstage center, or a light makes it seem so. The Chosen Ones' attentions are immediately caught by it.)*

BRAVE VOLUNTEER
We rested.

(The Chosen Ones tentatively move toward the fire and arrange themselves seated around it. They are seated, from SR to SL, The SON OF THE GODS, The BRAVE VOLUNTEER, The RELUCTANT BLOND, The SILENT PROTAGONIST, The ASS-KICKING TEEN, The BROODING HACKER. Things are becoming ceremonial; they are all staring into the fire as they speak.)

SILENT PROTAGONIST
I watched. And listened.

SON OF THE GODS
I remarked on our progress.

BROODING HACKER
I agreed. Begrudgingly.

BRAVE VOLUNTEER
I volunteered to take the first watch.

RELUCTANT BLOND
We agreed. But none of us could sleep yet.

BROODING HACKER
We were silent for a while.

(The Chosen Ones are silent for a moment.)

ASS-KICKING TEEN
I piped up and apologized.

(The other Chosen Ones look at her.)

BROODING HACKER

For what?

ASS-KICKING TEEN

Because of how I am. Because of the way my life has made me. I have to be the best, I have to be <u>perfect</u>. That's why I thought I was chosen. But I'm worried that if I keep going like this: perfect grades, perfect life, and saving the world... I'm gonna burn out before I even make it to college.

BROODING HACKER

I joked that college isn't all it's cracked up to be.

ASS-KICKING TEEN

I smiled.

BRAVE VOLUNTEER

I made a confession.

(The Chosen Ones' heads all snap in her direction.)

SILENT PROTAGONIST

(gently) What was it?

BRAVE VOLUNTEER

That my family's in danger because of me. I told you my story. Of how my town was taken over by a group of oligarchs who pitted citizens against each other for sport. I volunteered in order to keep my family safe, but they were imprisoned as collateral to keep me in line. I was a gladiator, killing for no reason, doing more harm in an effort to protect my family than I would if I just left and abandoned them. So I did. I refused to fight anymore, and I escaped.

ASS-KICKING TEEN
You have to know they'll forgive you. They're your family.

BRAVE VOLUNTEER
They denounced me on live television. Said I turned my
back on them. I could go try to rescue them, but they don't
want me to. That's why I'm always pushing forward, filling
my life with action and distractions. Even this, even trying to
save the world feels like a side quest. Feels like once I rescue
them, it'll all be over. Roll credits. They'll be free, but I'll
lose them. At least now I know where they are, and I know
that I can't put them in any more danger.

(The Chosen Ones' focuses all return to the fire.)

RELUCTANT BLOND
We were silent for a while.

BROODING HACKER
All internally reflecting on our own shortcomings.

SON OF THE GODS
On how I'll never ascend to godhood if I can't accept my
own mortality.

BROODING HACKER
On how I'll never save the world if I don't take help when
it's offered.

SILENT PROTAGONIST
On how I might never be heard. Seen. Understood.

RELUCTANT BLOND
On how I might never belong.

ASS-KICKING TEEN
We started to realize how much we have in common.

BROODING HACKER
Much more than our differences.

RELUCTANT BLOND
I remembered the flyer. I started to apologize.

BROODING HACKER
We wouldn't let you.

ASS-KICKING TEEN
Without you, we never would have found each other.

RELUCTANT BLOND
But what if it wasn't me? What if it was–

> *(The Chosen Ones all inhale and grasp their heads in pain.)*

SON OF THE GODS
We have faith in you. More than you have in yourself.

BRAVE VOLUNTEER
Besides, at least part of it was you.

BROODING HACKER. *(simultaneous)* "Bring snacks or something else to share."
ASS-KICKING TEEN. *(simultaneous)* "Bring snacks or something else to share."
SILENT PROTAGONIST. *(simultaneous)* "Bring snacks or something else to share."
RELUCTANT BLOND. *(simultaneous)* "Bring snacks or something else to share."
BRAVE VOLUNTEER. *(simultaneous)* "Bring snacks or something else to share."
SON OF THE GODS. *(simultaneous)* "Bring snacks or something else to share."

ASS-KICKING TEEN

We all smiled.

BROODING HACKER

And a companionable silence melted into a pestering fear.

RELUCTANT BLOND

There were things we wanted to say, but we didn't yet know how.

SON OF THE GODS

We'll die if we choose wrong.

BRAVE VOLUNTEER

Will we?

RELUCTANT BLOND

Won't we?

BROODING HACKER

But we know the path ahead.

ASS-KICKING TEEN

Do we?

SON OF THE GODS

Don't we?

SILENT PROTAGONIST

(reciting with great reverence) "For as long as there have been forces of creation, there have also been forces of destruction. One day there will arise a power not only capable of destruction, but able to end the very act of creation itself. And against that power, a hero shall rise! The power will be known by its desire for silence. And the hero

PROTAGONIST (cont)
will be known by the company they keep. And should that
hero fail, the power will rule, and everything shall end."

RELUCTANT BLOND
(calmly) Everything?

SILENT PROTAGONIST
"Everything. And when the power shall first show its face,
the true hero will falter.

RELUCTANT BLOND
What does that mean?

ASS-KICKING TEEN
We refused the call. We weren't perfect.

RELUCTANT BLOND
I refused it more than anyone else. Is it me?

SON OF THE GODS
We've all had our doubts. But you're still in the running.

SILENT PROTAGONIST
"But by their rise, events shall be put into motion unseen and
unknown. A mountain must be climbed, both of earth and of
the mind."

BRAVE VOLUNTEER
Check.

SILENT PROTAGONIST
"For a party shall be formed of strangers who become
friends."

RELUCTANT BLOND
Check.

SILENT PROTAGONIST
"And they shall seek out a series of old men who shall aid in their efforts, each with a beard that is longer and whiter than the last."

BROODING HACKER
Definitely check.

ASS-KICKING TEEN
I wouldn't call one old man a series.

BROODING HACKER
We've got time.

SILENT PROTAGONIST
"And at the eleventh second of the eleventh minute of the eleventh hour of the eleventh day of the eleventh week of the eleventh month of the eleventh year of the eleventh era, The Chosen One will rise. And the day shall truly be saved.

BROODING HACKER
So it was...

ASS-KICKING TEEN
...is...

BRAVE VOLUNTEER
...and forever will be."

(They sit in silence for a moment in reflection of The Prophecy.)

SON OF THE GODS
When is that? The eleventh era and stuff?

BROODING HACKER
I'm not sure that that's for us to know.

SILENT PROTAGONIST
Soon.

ASS-KICKING TEEN
Feels soon.

BRAVE VOLUNTEER
Feels…cold.

BROODING HACKER
Fire's going down.

(The fire is indeed starting to fade.)

RELUCTANT BLOND
Sun's coming up.

(The sunlight is indeed starting to rise.)

SON OF THE GODS
And we wake up.

RELUCTANT BLOND
But we're not where we were.

ASS-KICKING TEEN
Where were we?

BRAVE VOLUNTEER
In the forest outside of The Overthinker's fortress.

(The Chosen Ones all realize with a gasp that they can think and say his name.)

BROODING HACKER. *(simultaneous)* The Overthinker.
ASS-KICKING TEEN. *(simultaneous)* The Overthinker.
SILENT PROTAGONIST. *(simultaneous)* The Overthinker.
RELUCTANT BLOND. *(simultaneous)* The Overthinker.
BRAVE VOLUNTEER. *(simultaneous)* The Overthinker.
SON OF THE GODS. *(simultaneous)* The Overthinker.

RELUCTANT BLOND

If we can say his name, he's real.

BRAVE VOLUNTEER

If he's real, we can find him.

SON OF THE GODS

If we can find him, we're not done fighting.

SILENT PROTAGONIST

If we're not done fighting, we're in danger....

> *(The bell dings again SL. We hear the sound of footsteps. The Chosen Ones all turn to face the door and ready their crouched battle positions. After a moment of tension, The BOY WIZARD enters again.)*

BOY WIZARD

Sorry, I just wanted to double-check, cause the sign says that you're open–

BROODING HACKER. *(simultaneous)* GET LOST, MAGIC BOY, WE DON'T WANT–
ASS-KICKING TEEN. *(simultaneous)* IF YOU BREATHE ONE MORE NERDY BREATH–
SILENT PROTAGONIST. *(simultaneous)* YOU ARE NOT A PART OF THIS–
RELUCTANT BLOND. *(simultaneous)* WE'RE NOT OPEN TO YOU SO STOP ASKING–

BRAVE VOLUNTEER. *(simultaneous)* HOW DARE YOU
IMPOSE UPON THIS–
SON OF THE GODS. *(simultaneous)* I WILL CALL UPON
THE ELEMENTS TO RIP YOU–

RELUCTANT BLOND
(rising suddenly) Wait! This nerd is not our enemy.

BROODING HACKER
He's right. We've got to find The Overthinker.

ASS-KICKING TEEN
And bring him down!

SON OF THE GODS
But how? We're trapped in this false reality.

SILENT PROTAGONIST
Not trapped. Stripped of our actual selves.

BROODING HACKER
Then we have to get ourselves back!

BRAVE VOLUNTEER
Back from those who volunteered us in the first place!

SILENT PROTAGONIST
Yes! In the liminal space where we were all introduced and
given our potential!

BOY WIZARD
Do you guys need help?

RELUCTANT BLOND
Not from you, nerd!!

ASS-KICKING TEEN

We'll get back to normal, head back to the fortress, and stop
The Overthinker once and for all!

BROODING HACKER

Let's go!

*(The Chosen Ones scurry, leaving their TTRPG
stuff behind and pushing past The BOY WIZARD
as they exit SL. The BOY WIZARD stands alone
for a moment. He observes the shop as he
approaches the front counter. In a fit of anger, he
picks up the GM screen and smashes it over and
over again, scattering paper and pencil and
dice. As he breathes in the aftermath of his
destruction, The FANATIC pops up from behind
the counter.)*

FANATIC

We could help each other, sweetness. Ahem! Ahem!

(The BOY WIZARD smiles. Blackout.)

SCENE VI

Inside The Overthinker's Fortress.

A throne room. There is a grand throne SL. The rest of the room is decorated as time and budget permits. Most importantly, The BOY WIZARD is seated on the throne, and The OVERTHINKER lays sprawled on the ground upstage center.

The Chosen Ones rush on from SR. They are no longer "normal," but maybe aren't as entirely kitted out as they were before, just with the key elements of their archetypes.

SON OF THE GODS

We're back!

BROODING HACKER

Everyone feeling like yourself again?

ASS-KICKING TEEN

Better than ever!

RELUCTANT BLOND

In B&B parlance…I think we finally leveled up.

SILENT PROTAGONIST

Hup! Hyah!!

BROODING HACKER

Glad to hear it.

BRAVE VOLUNTEER

Now let's finish off The Overthinker once and for all!

MENTOR

(calling out from off-stage right) Not so fast!

(The Chosen Ones whirl around to look at The MENTOR as he enters, staff aloft, his beard longer and whiter than ever before. His skin is also a sort of sickly greenish gray.)

SON OF THE GODS

By the Rod of Asclepius! One of our greatest allies has been turned against us!

MENTOR

What? No, I just meant, like, don't go in without me, I can't walk that fast.

(The MENTOR's hands fall off, his staff clattering to the ground still gripped in one of them.)

MENTOR

And I'm fallin' apart, gosh darn it.

(The MENTOR stoops to try and retrieve his hands. The Chosen Ones move in and help him reattach them.)

ASS-KICKING TEEN

What happened to you?

MENTOR

"Death is just another path, one that we all must take." Being <u>un</u>dead however, that sucks. The Overthinker killed me, but The Powers That Be decided my task was not finished so...

(The MENTOR gestures at himself and his hand falls off again. One of The Chosen Ones helps him retrieve it.)

BRAVE VOLUNTEER

If they thought you were important enough to save from death…perhaps <u>you</u> are The Chosen One afterall.

MENTOR

Nah, they lost a bet a few centuries ago and owed me a one-up. It's still up to one of you…if any of you are still willing to stand up to the call.

> *(The Chosen Ones look at each other and have assembled themselves into some kind of presentational cluster once more. After checking in and mentally agreeing, they nod.)*

ASS-KICKING TEEN

We are.

SON OF THE GODS

More ready than we've ever been.

BRAVE VOLUNTEER

And even more ready when we're together.

SILENT PROTAGONIST

Heeah!

RELUCTANT BLOND

(to The BROODING HACKER) What d'you say? One final snarky quip for the road?

BROODING HACKER

(with a grin and a pose) It's time to take that villain down or die trying. *(lowering his shades dramatically)* And I'm all out of dying.

RELUCTANT BLOND

Overthinker! Your time has– *(clocking the scene before them)* Whoa, what the heck is going on here?

BOY WIZARD

Oh, that? The Overthinker and I had a little chat and I defeated him. Threat eliminated. Problem solved.

BROODING HACKER

Y-...you defeated him?

ASS-KICKING TEEN

With magic?

SON OF THE GODS

Or the power of friendship?

BOY WIZARD

Nnnno, with a bat to the back of the head.

BROODING HACKER. *(simultaneous)* Where did you get a bat? I thought you had a wand.
ASS-KICKING TEEN. *(simultaneous)* Oooh, yeah, I've defeated a monster or two that way.
SILENT PROTAGONIST. *(simultaneous)* Hm. Huh. Hup. Hrm.
RELUCTANT BLOND. *(simultaneous)* Oh gosh. Is he…? When you say "defeated."
BRAVE VOLUNTEER. *(simultaneous)* Not exactly poetic, but I guess it works.
SON OF THE GODS. *(simultaneous)* I was going to use the powers of the gods, but that works.
MENTOR. *(simultaneous)* Aw, c'mon, man, that seems needlessly gratuitous.

BRAVE VOLUNTEER

But he–

BOY WIZARD

He's not important anymore. You all were paying him <u>far</u> too much attention, but now that he's gone, we can get back to what really matters. **Me**!

ASS-KICKING TEEN

What's going on? How did you even get in here?

(The FANATIC pops up from behind the throne.)

FANATIC

Hello!

BROODING HACKER. *(simultaneous)* Ahem!
ASS-KICKING TEEN. *(simultaneous)* Ahem!
SILENT PROTAGONIST. *(simultaneous)* Hiyah!
RELUCTANT BLOND. *(simultaneous)* Ahem!
BRAVE VOLUNTEER. *(simultaneous)* Ahem!
SON OF THE GODS. *(simultaneous)* Ahem!

BOY WIZARD

Excuse me?

BROODING HACKER

There **is** no excuse for you, twerp. *(to The FANATIC)* Ahem, what are you doing here?

FANATIC

We helped the boy wizard find a shortcut. And a bat.

MENTOR

(advancing menacingly on The FANATIC) I told you what was going to happen the next time I saw you, you little freak—

(Mid-approach, The MENTOR's hands fall off again.)

MENTOR

Aw, gosh **dang** it!

(The MENTOR stoops to pick up his hands and the nearest Chosen Ones try to help too, but he shoos them away.)

MENTOR

Let me do it, let me do it on my own. *(muttering as he tries)* I'll never learn unless I do it on my own. A lesson you all might have learned the first time instead of following *(gesturing as best he can at The FANATIC)* this freak up the mountain.

(Everyone stands for a moment and watches The MENTOR struggle.)

ASS-KICKING TEEN

(turning back to The FANATIC) But why, Ahem? Why help him? He's so <u>annoying</u>.

FANATIC

People think <u>I'm</u> annoying too…

(The Chosen Ones shift with various awkward reactions, hands in pockets, kicking the ground, that kind of thing.)

BROODING HACKER. *(simultaneous)* That's not <u>exactly</u> the word that I would use…
ASS-KICKING TEEN. *(simultaneous)* Oh, c'mon, no one said that, did they…?
SILENT PROTAGONIST. *(simultaneous)*
Urrrrrrrrrrrrrrrm….

RELUCTANT BLOND. *(simultaneous)* Sticks and stones, you know, you gotta…

BRAVE VOLUNTEER. *(simultaneous)* Annoying is in the eye of the beholder…

SON OF THE GODS. *(simultaneous)* I mean, I was <u>thinking</u> it, but not out loud…

MENTOR

(still struggling) I do. I think you're **really** annoying, you little freak.

BOY WIZARD

(roaring) Silence!!

(The Chosen Ones react with fear.)

BOY WIZARD

This isn't about him. And it isn't about any of you. It's about **<u>me</u>**! It was always supposed to be about **<u>ME</u>**! I'm the best boy there ever **<u>was</u>**!!

BROODING HACKER

That's your problem, you know that? I'll admit, you <u>used</u> to be pretty cool. But now, you can't tell the difference between good attention and bad attention. We know from experience that there's a long road between who a person was and who they become. And who you've become is a real loser. You jerk! You bully! You…nobody!

BOY WIZARD

Oh yeah? Is that the way you wanna play it? Well, I've got a few snarky **<u>quips</u>** of my own.

(The BOY WIZARD pulls out his wand and aims it at The Chosen Ones.)

BOY WIZARD
(casting a spell) IWANNACANNOLI!

> *(The Chosen Ones cry out in pain, muscles
> seizing and clenching as the magic strikes them.)*

BRAVE VOLUNTEER
(pleading; to The MENTOR) You've got to do something!

MENTOR
I don't even have my hands on yet!!

> *(The BOY WIZARD strikes again.)*

BOY WIZARD
IGOTTAGOPOTTY!

> *(The Chosen Ones cry out in pain once more.
> The FANATIC watches uncomfortably as The
> BOY WIZARD cackles with glee.)*

ASS-KICKING TEEN
(gritting her teeth through the pain) Ahem…please…help
us….

> *(The BOY WIZARD zaps them again.)*

BOY WIZARD
IBOUGHTAFERRARI!

> *(The Chosen Ones writhe in pain.)*

RELUCTANT BLOND
(through pleading tears; to The FANATIC) …you can be…
the hero…too!

(The FANATIC has a moment of internal conflict before leaping onto The BOY WIZARD's back and attacking him. The BOY WIZARD's concentration on the spell is broken.)

BOY WIZARD

What are you–??

(The FANATIC continues attacking The BOY WIZARD, eventually latching onto The BOY WIZARD's wand hand. He bites off a finger and the wand falls to the floor.)

BOY WIZARD

My finger!! You bit off my bloody finger! And now it's a bloody finger!

(The FANATIC spits out the finger and releases The BOY WIZARD. The BOY WIZARD clutches his hand in pain and stumbles away from the throne.)

BOY WIZARD

You…miserable little creature. How dare you presume upon my story? **I** am the central character. The Chosen One **and** the destructive force. Protagonist, deuteragonist, tritagonist, the trinity all-in-one! I am franchise and spin-off! I am merchandise and subsidiary! I–

(The FANATIC climbs up the throne.)

FANTATIC

You talk too much.

(The FANATIC pushes the throne backward onto The BOY WIZARD.)

BOY WIZARD

Noooooooo!

> *(The throne falls with a mighty THUD and crushes The BOY WIZARD, who lies defeated under it. The Chosen Ones celebrate and gather around The FANATIC.)*

BROODING HACKER. *(simultaneous)* Wow, I did not see that coming.

ASS-KICKING TEEN. *(simultaneous)* Ahem, you did it! You saved us!

SILENT PROTAGONIST. *(simultaneous)* Hyah hep! Hyyaaahh!

RELUCTANT BLOND. *(simultaneous)* Now <u>that</u> was a critical success!

BRAVE VOLUNTEER. *(simultaneous)* Well done, brave, strange warrior!

SON OF THE GODS. *(simultaneous)* This might be my first ever thank you!

> *(The celebration stops as The Chosen Ones realize The FANATIC's breathing is heavy. He is dying.)*

FANATIC

(coughing up blood) <u>Ahem</u>, <u>ahem</u>.

ASS-KICKING TEEN

Ahem?

BROODING HACKER

What's wrong?

FANATIC

Dying, sweetness.

SON OF THE GODS
What? How?

RELUCTANT BLOND
Did he hit you with a spell?

FANATIC
Boy wizard's blood was…<u>ahem</u>, too toxic. Poisoned us, sweetness.

BRAVE VOLUNTEER
(at The BOY WIZARD's body) Will his cruelties never cease?

SON OF THE GODS
We must do something!

MENTOR
I'm afraid…there's nothing we can do. The little freak's time has come.

ASS-KICKING TEEN
(with firm resolve) Then a remembrance…for a fallen companion. How can we honor your legacy, Ahem?

RELUCTANT BLOND
We could…at least start calling him by his actual name.

ASS-KICKING TEEN
That's true…. *(to The FANATIC)* I'm sorry we didn't learn it sooner. What is your name, friend?

> *(The FANATIC coughs once or twice before summoning the strength to respond.)*

FANATIC

That is kind, sweetness. Friends call friends by friends' name. ...my name is... *(The FANATIC says his name, but it's just a big long spill of blurbing consonants because he's dying)* Buhlllbgbluhgblglllbl....

(The Chosen Ones share a look.)

ASS-KICKING TEEN

Sorry, what was it?

FANATIC

(more insistent and somehow less comprehensible) Bluhllhhglblbllbllhgbl.

RELUCTANT BLOND

Does anyone have a pen or–?

(The FANATIC dies with a blurbling of sounds.)

BROODING HACKER

Oh, he's dead.

(The Chosen Ones mourn in a moment of confusion.)

ASS-KICKING TEEN

Okay, so.

BROODING HACKER

So then, wait, was that–...? Are we–...?

BRAVE VOLUNTEER

Is evil defeated? Did one of us do it?

SON OF THE GODS
(of The FANATIC) Also, we're not gonna call him that, right? We'll just keep calling him Ahem, right?

MENTOR
If The Overthinker was the big bad, then boy wizard there was The Chosen One.

BRAVE VOLUNTEER
Capital C, capital O.

ASS-KICKING TEEN
But if boy wizard was the big bad, then... *(thinking back to the name)* ...then Ahem was The Chosen One.

BROODING HACKER
Capital A, capital Hem.

RELUCTANT BLOND
But that's all if...and I hate that this is such a really big 'if', but...if The Overthinker is actually....

> *(The Chosen Ones all slowly turn to look at The OVERTHINKER's body. It doesn't move. Satisfied, The Chosen Ones all turn back to the group.)*

BROODING HACKER
Okay, good that would have been–

> *(The Chosen Ones all quickly whip their heads back in the direction of The OVERTHINKER's body. It doesn't move. They are all very suspicious but slowly turn back to the group.)*

BROODING HACKER
I could have sworn he was gonna–

ASS-KICKING TEEN
–jump up and go 'Aha, I fooled you!', right?

RELUCTANT BLOND
Villains love to do that.

MENTOR
(agreeing) Villains <u>love</u> to do that.

SON OF THE GODS
Are we sure he's…hold on.

> *(The SON OF THE GODS moves cautiously over to The OVERTHINKER's body. He examines it for a moment, then pokes it. It doesn't move. The SON OF THE GODS pokes it tentatively, then rolls the body over. He realizes and hoists it up.)*

SON OF THE GODS
Guys, it's fake!

BROODING HACKER
What?

> *(The SON OF THE GODS lifts the body over his head and lets it flop around.)*

SON OF THE GODS
The Overthinker's body. It's just a dummy. See?

BRAVE VOLUNTEER
Huh.

BROODING HACKER
But then that would mean….

ASS-KICKING TEEN
But why would…?

> *(From beneath the throne, The BOY WIZARD
> starts laughing. It is a low rumble that builds
> into a vaulting cacophony. The Chosen Ones
> back away in a strategic group as The BOY
> WIZARD rises, pressing the throne off of him
> and pushing it aside.)*

BOY WIZARD
Did you miss me?

SON OF THE GODS
No, not at all actually!

BROODING HACKER
If you zap us again, I will <u>end</u> you.

RELUCTANT BLOND
Why does <u>he</u> get to come back from the dead??

BOY WIZARD
(teasing) Perhaps it was my **<u>destiny</u>**.

BROODING HACKER
How many times do we have to tell you? You're **not** The
Chosen One; one of **us** is.

BRAVE VOLUNTEER
Or all of us are.

SON OF THE GODS
Or none of us are, it actually <u>is</u> still kinda confusing.

BOY WIZARD

SILENCE! I–

ASS-KICKING TEEN

Wait!!!

(All eyes turn on The ASS-KICKING TEEN.)

ASS-KICKING TEEN
(with the most import with which these three words have ever been uttered) Say. That. Again.

(The BOY WIZARD does, and when he does it is a terrifying, slithering whisper, a primordial oozing of the villain's true intentions.

BOY WIZARD
(smiling) Silence.

ASS-KICKING TEEN
It's you! You're the destructive power!

BROODING HACKER
What?

ASS-KICKING TEEN
(quoting) "The power will be known by its desire for silence." It's you. You've been the villain this whole time.

RELUCTANT BLOND
How is that possible?

BOY WIZARD
(now a toothy, cunning antagonist) What? Did you think the ultimate destructive force, foretold by time itself, would wear but one mask? Would bear but one shape?

RELUCTANT BLOND
You're The Overthinker?

BOY WIZARD
I go by many names. The Liar. The Judge. The Turncoat….

> *(The BOY WIZARD smiles wickedly, looking*
> *past The Chosen Ones. The Chosen Ones follow*
> *his gaze and see The MENTOR standing*
> *handless and despondent.)*

MENTOR
I'm so sorry…

> *(The MENTOR reveals his real hands from*
> *within his sleeves and zaps The Chosen Ones*
> *who react with fear and pain.)*

BOY WIZARD
I have laid every shadow beneath every step you have taken.
Carved the footprints in stone that led straight to your doom.

SON OF THE GODS
But why?

BOY WIZARD
Why?? For SILENCE!

> *(The MENTOR stops zapping and the silence is*
> *stark.)*

BOY WIZARD
Everything new only gets in my way. When I have finally
silenced every voice, destroyed every act of creation, there
will finally be peace. There will finally be stillness. No
judgement. No criticism. It will be me alone. At the center of
everything. Unchanging. Unafraid. Forever.

BROODING HACKER
(panting through the pain) You're missing the point, kid.

BOY WIZARD
Of what, pray tell?

BROODING HACKER
Of life. If you can't see that, you're beyond help.

BOY WIZARD
Well…at least we can agree on something. *(to The MENTOR)* Finish them.

(The MENTOR zaps The Chosen Ones again and they writhe in agony and the anguish of impending defeat.)

BOY WIZARD
And now <u>nothing</u> can stand in my way!

BRAVE VOLUNTEER
(through gritted teeth) We can still…stop him!

SON OF THE GODS
We can't! We never could! He **is** The Chosen One!

BROODING HACKER
No!

RELUCTANT BLOND
Of course he is! He's been in control of everything this whole **time**! Every enemy we faced, every mentor we thought we could trust! Probably even the customer in the comic book store on the day when we all first met!

(The MENTOR stops zapping and The BOY WIZARD stops laughing.)

BOY WIZARD

Wait, what? No, that wasn't–

(With a crash of triumphant music, The CUSTOMER breaks through the wall and enters heroically with an army of GRUNTS.)

CUSTOMER

I brought something to share!!

(The GRUNTs overtake the stage. They surround The MENTOR, corralling him offstage right.)

MENTOR

No, wait, this is my last liiiiiiife….!

(The Chosen Ones turn on The BOY WIZARD.)

ASS-KICKING TEEN

That just leaves one more butt to kick.

(There is a final climactic battle sequence where each Chosen One gets in a final, character-defining piece of choreography. The final move is by The CUSTOMER, who slices The BOY WIZARD's throat with a comic book, tossing it aside. The BOY WIZARD gurgles and falls.)

RELUCTANT BLOND

(to The BOY WIZARD) That'll teach you to damage store property.

ASS-KICKING TEEN
*(putting a hand on his shoulder to observe The BOY
WIZARD's body)* Now **that** was a hell of a quippy one-liner.

(The RELUCTANT BLOND blushes.)

BRAVE VOLUNTEER
(to The CUSTOMER) But how did you find us?

CUSTOMER
I followed the hidden instructions in your flyer. *(to The
RELUCTANT BLOND)* Great ARG, by the way.

RELUCTANT BLOND
Wh–what do you mean?

CUSTOMER
You know. "The stars have foretold your arrival." I followed
the North Star to this old fort. "Will you answer the call?" I
found the Grunts in the forest and learned their language.
"Come rescue the Damsel of Lucerna Lake." That was easy,
that's you guys needing rescuing. And then, "The fate of the
story rests in your ready hands." I figured landing the killing
blow with a comic book would be some kind of poetic
justice. Oh, and "Bring your own snacks or something to
share." I figured that was either a backdoor into figuring out
The Grunts or just a red herring.

BROODING HACKER
So while we were worrying about The Prophecy–

ASS-KICKING TEEN
– Capital T, capital P –

RELUCTANT BLOND
–it turns out there was a whole other lowercase prophecy we
hadn't even considered.

95

SON OF THE GODS
A prophetic turducken.

RELUCTANT BLOND
Maybe I had a little more influence over the original messaging than I realized.

BRAVE VOLUNTEER
That or The Overthinker overthought his way into his own demise.

BROODING HACKER
(to The CUSTOMER) So wait, then are **you** The Chosen One?

RELUCTANT BLOND
(of The CUSTOMER) Is that why he was there when The Overthinker gathered us?

SON OF THE GODS
This is getting ridiculous! Maybe there's no such **thing** as a Chosen One!

ASS-KICKING TEEN
No, I refuse to believe that after all we've been through. It has to be one of us, right?

BRAVE VOLUNTEER
It has to be. It **has** to be. *(shouting to the heavens)* Which one of us is The Chosen One??

(The Powers That Be enter variously.)

PTB 1
You <u>all</u> are.

BROODING HACKER. *(simultaneous)* Huh?
ASS-KICKING TEEN. *(simultaneous)* Huh?
SILENT PROTAGONIST. *(simultaneous)* Huh?
RELUCTANT BLOND. *(simultaneous)* Huh?
BRAVE VOLUNTEER. *(simultaneous)* Huh?
SON OF THE GODS. *(simultaneous)* Huh?

CUSTOMER

How?

PTB 2

We don't know. And it's about time we fessed up to that.

PTB 3

The whole of reality is big and weird and really hard to keep track of.

PTB 1

So sometimes things don't turn out the way we think they will. Or hope they will. Or want them to.

RELUCTANT BLOND

Is that…satisfying?

PTB 1

For a story? Maybe. For life? That's not the point.

SON OF THE GODS

Were we good at what we did?

PTB 3

You were the best. Literally perfect.

BRAVE VOLUNTEER

And it couldn't have happened without us?

PTB 2

Well, in a way. But that's true of everyone and everything. A story changes depending on who's telling it, who's watching it, why it's being told.

RELUCTANT BLOND

And what happens to us now?

PTB 1

Well, your paths continue. In here, out there. However you choose. Your life becomes a story worth reading in a world worth saving.

BROODING HACKER

It's over, then? Just like that?

PTB

Just like that.

ASS-KICKING TEEN

What if we never see each other again? What if our paths don't intertwine?

PTB 2

They might. You never really know. But you'll always have your memories. And that…well, sometimes that has to be enough.

RELUCTANT BLOND

Then I guess…this is goodbye.

PTB 3

Yeah. This is goodbye. At least…until the sequel.

(PTB 3 winks at the audience as The Powers That Be snap their fingers. The snap is amplified to be impossibly loud. Blackout.)

END

www.ingramcontent.com/pod-product-compliance
Lightning Source LLC
Chambersburg PA
CBHW020323130626
46549CB00003B/989